A Nutty World
on the Edge of the Rain Forest

By Rita Lossett   Illustrated by Teri Hoffman

Copyright © 2023 Rita Lossett.

All rights reserved. No part of this book may be reproduced, stored, or transmitted by any means—whether auditory, graphic, mechanical, or electronic—without written permission of both publisher and author, except in the case of brief excerpts used in critical articles and reviews. Unauthorized reproduction of any part of this work is illegal and is punishable by law.

ISBN: 979-8-89031-270-9 (sc)
ISBN: 979-8-89031-271-6 (hc)
ISBN: 979-8-89031-272-3 (e)

Because of the dynamic nature of the Internet, any web addresses or links contained in this book may have changed since publication and may no longer be valid. The views expressed in this work are solely those of the author and do not necessarily reflect the views of the publisher, and the publisher hereby disclaims any responsibility for them.

One Galleria Blvd., Suite 1900, Metairie, LA 70001
1-888-421-2397

A Nutty World on the Edge of the Rain Forest
is dedicated to all who find a connection
to nature in their world.

South America

Can you find Brazil on a map of South America?

Brazil nut trees grow on the edge of the rain forests. Some trees can live to be over a thousand years old.

Some have grown 150 feet tall—that's as tall as the Statue of Liberty!

Brazil nuts are natural products from the rain forest. Humans did not plant the trees. But humans do need them! Brazil nut trees provide healthy food and jobs for thousands of people who live on the edge of the rain forest.

What do Brazil nut trees need?

The Brazil nut trees find the perfect habitat on the edge of the forest. There is light and space to grow and not too much rain. Brazil nut trees like to dry out for four or five months every year.

These old giants of the forest depend on animals and insects and flowers to survive. Their habitat needs to be protected because the edge of the forest is being cleared and cut down for more farming and industry.

Have you ever tried to open a Brazil nut?

It takes muscle!

Sitting high in the old trees are red-faced uakaris. The hungry monkeys have long sharp incisors and strong jaw muscles to rip open Brazil nut pods.

The ripe pods are the size of a baseball, and they are filled with tempting nuts at the end of the rainy season.

The quick hands of a uakari scoop out 10 to 15 nuts for a tasty treat.

They throw the empty pods 100 or more feet to the ground where other ripe pods have already fallen.

Look for ripe pods.

Did the monkeys miss any?

Watch out, harvesters! Don't get hit in the head. A ripe pod filled with nuts can weigh five pounds.

Don't step on the agouti! The rabbit-sized rodents on the forest floor are quietly looking for the pods, too.

The pods have a small hole at one end. It allows the agoutis long chiseled teeth and strong jaw muscle to pry open the pods and crack the nuts open. Agoutis love munching on the nuts. When they have had enough, they carry some away to bury in a shady spot to save for a future meal.

Where did I put that nut? wonders the agouti. This is how Brazil nut trees are planted.

It is the agouti that does it!!

The rains come again. If the agouti can't remember where the nuts are buried, new Brazil nut trees will slowly begin to grow. The little trees wait in the shade for an old giant to fall allowing sunlight for the little ones to grow.

Nothing is wasted at the edge of the rain forest. The empty pods will be used again. Tiny Brazil nut frogs no bigger than a thumbnail find them just right to protect their tadpoles. The female frog lays her eggs on the ground. The male frog guards the eggs. When they hatch, he carries the tadpoles to an empty pod.

Rain water has collected at the bottom of the pod. The tadpoles grow quickly. They have an all-you-can-eat buffet from the larvae of mosquitoes and other insects that have hatched in the water in the Brazil nut pod.

After the rains, yellow flowers bloom high in the Brazil nut trees. Each flower makes tiny grains of pollen. Only one kind of bee can spread the pollen from flower to flower to create a new crop of nuts—a female orchid bee.

Orchid bees are not like other bees. They don't live in a hive. They work alone. They are attracted to the smell of orchid flowers growing on the forest floor.

Orchid bees don't like to buzz too far to find food. Not only do they love the rich nectar from the orchids, but they also need the sweet treat waiting for them in the yellow flowers growing on the Brazil nut trees.

Each buttery yellow flower has a well of sweet nectar protected by a coiled, arched hood. The bee has a long, strong tongue that can lift the hood. She collects the nectar with her tongue. Now she has energy! Tiny pollen sticks to her to legs and drops off when she buzzes from flower to flower.

The male orchid bee is too small to do any heavy lifting. He buzzes around the orchid flowers to perfume himself to attract the females flying nearby. At the same time, he is spreading tiny grains of pollen among the orchid flowers too.

In 15 months, instead of flowers there will be new pods filled with Brazil nuts hanging from the Brazil nut trees. The nutty web of connections will repeat again on the edge of the rain forest.

The Brazil nut trees need the monkeys and agoutis. These towering, old giants need the orchid flowers and the tiny bees. The bees and the frogs, the monkeys and agoutis, the orchids and the humans all need the trees. Without each other, they can NUT survive!

Did you know . . .

. . . pacas also compete with agoutis for Brazil nuts on the forest floor?

. . . the scientific name for a red-faced uakari is *Cacajao calvus,* pronounced ka-ka-ha-o cal-vus?

. . . Brazil nut harvesters are called *castanheiros* in Portuguese?

. . . the oil from Brazil nuts is used for making artists' paints?

. . . Brazil nut trees grow in other countries besides Brazil? They also grow in Peru, Venezuela, the Guianas, parts of Colombia and Bolivia.

. . . in one year, a Brazil nut tree can produce 250 pounds of nuts?

. . . the red face of a uakari (pronounced oo-a-ka-ree) is not caused by a sun burn? It is born that way.

. . . the Brazil nut contains protein, calcium, iron and zinc?

. . . you can find connections all around your world, too?

Teri Hoffman is a biological and medical illustrator who earned degrees in Biological Illustration and in Botany through UCLA and California State University, Long Beach. She is also a docent at the Los Angeles Zoo and Botanical Gardens, leading tours for youngsters, families and college-aged students. She finds her connections through these activities and the animals and plants that populate the world.